sharp notes

Idalis Payne

BookLeaf Publishing

India | USA | UK

Presentation by *BookLeaf Publishing*

Web: www.bookleafpub.com

E-mail: info@bookleafpub.com

ISBN: 9789358316971

First edition 2023

DEDICATION

to linda, grammy, papa, and tommy. thank you.
for everything.

bloom

the sun
shines
after a
storm

the arch of
a rainbow
peeks
through the clouds

the thought
of you
escapes me.

the sun
kisses
my skin

memories
of you
fading.

i took
the long
way home

and sometimes
i think if
had i not met
you

i wouldn't
have
been able to
bloom.

try

there are times when
i lay
in bed
i can feel
my heartbeat
pulsating
through
my teeth
my limbs
are tense
my stomach
roars

i wonder what the next day
will bring

my mind
wanders
to the past
i can't help
but think
"what is wrong with me?"

will i be able to exist without
the need

to feel
seen?
loved?
encouraged?

in a way that's so
pure
so
wholesome

that even when
the skies
are gray
i still make the
choice
to
try

outside

i often feel as if
everyone is
in
a glass house
and i have
no way
in

people are
laughing and
smiling and
hugging and
kissing and
warmth can be felt
but i have
no way
in

my frosty breath
is
my only friend
my chest
tightens and
my eyes
burn

i'm stuck
on the outside
with
no way
in

shadow

i wish
my brain
was my friend
do you know how
exhausting
it is to be
sad?
all the time?

to have nightmares?
while awake?
and only ever cry?

my brain is not my friend
i wish that it would end

the voices in my head say

"you're better off dead"
"that no one really loves me"

i try so hard to be happy
but i fall short
in the end

i break
my heart
each evening
wondering if
love really wins

i didn't ask for this
the pain that persists
becoming my own shadow
impossible to resist

you are loved

i hope you know you are loved
i hope you know
that in the brief moments when the sun awakens
and kisses the ocean good morning
there is someone in the world who hopes
that you had a good night's rest

i hope you know
that to them
you are a star in their solar system
one that they look up to
every day

and spend countless minutes,
maybe even hours
hoping that they'll spot you
that you made your return
with a warmth so bright

i hope you know
they pray you never burn out
that even on the cloudiest of nights
when not even the north star is in sight
they can still feel you
your energy above

i hope you know
you are loved

i love you?

what if i told you
that i loved you?
that the thought of seeing
your name
light up on my phone screen
sent small jolts of hope
through my body?
made me think that perhaps
you could be
the one
not just because of the small things
but the big ones, too
through all that was happening
i still wanted
you
but after some time
i realized
that you didn't
want me
in the same way
i thought you needed me
and i never said
i love you
because
you
didn't love me

seen

i thought i saw your face again today
nearly panicked
didn't know quite what to say
then relief washed over me
as i realized my brain
was foolin' on me

i couldn't help but wonder
what could be
if i'd seen you
and you'd seen me

would we finally say what was on our minds?
or would we both turn away and hide?

why is it so hard to say how we really feel?
why isn't the truth easily revealed?

why do we play games when the score stays the
same?
and in overtime
no one ends up winning

wonder

you cross my mind more often
than i'd like to admit
like a strong gust of wind
barreling me over
or a wave crashing down
on my skin
i wonder if i ever do the same
to you

miss me?

14

clouds dance in the sky
raindrops glisten in my eyes
do you miss me now?

nightmares

15

the horrors wake me and the
dreams deceive me and now
my heart is racing

tears

16

saltwater streaming down my face
my eyes are an ocean at war with itself
my runny nose sounds like an angry seashell
and my headache pounds like thunder
the darkness behind my eyelids beg for a
peaceful end

you

i would much rather be
a fool
who advocates for
herself
rather than
a person
who loves condescension
and telling others
how to behave
it must feel nice for you
to have so much power
that you wield it recklessly
and doubt my own abilities
yet you were the one who
left early
without much grace
from what i heard
isn't it funny
that you became
your own enemy?

words

why am i never good enough?
why can't i just be?

i wonder what it's like to be chosen
and not feel lonely

are the words you say
what you really think of me?

maybe i am soft
and too sensitive
maybe i'm the one
who's trying to tell you
how it is

can't you please hear me out?
i wish we could agree

the words you say have more meaning
than you could ever see

walk away

could you come
say you want me more
i fell in love with you

the night comes
you walk away
i begged you to stay

you sit there
blankly stare
get up and
walk away

remembering

do you think
a memory
is worth
remembering
even once your
heart
says
let go
when your
brain
gives you
every logical reason
to say
goodbye?

when those two worlds
align
are they sending
a sign?

how do you
let go
when you
swore you knew
it would never end?

neon

you were neon
i was a dimly-lit candle
one you'd find at a big box store
your neon lights burned much too bright
and i held on for too long
my light burned out
and now it's time to
move on.

bandage

22

orange bottle
blue lid
white pill

saltwater streams
depression memes

bandages to mask
my feral pain

taste

i hate i changed
the shape of me
when you had
somebody waiting

she's pretty
and i'm sure
she's great

but does she know
that you know
how i taste?

questions

we never said what was needed
only silence filled the air
a guessing game
and no time
to spare

i stuck around too long
but now that i'm here
i have a few things i'd like to say

how is it you were dishonest
and still got your happy ending?

was i just a notch on your belt?

did it mean anything?
did you have something to prove?
did you get what you wanted?

do you care that we don't talk?
do you regret it?

are you happy
or are you sad?

am i your worst nightmare
or your best daydream?

and when you read this
will you think of me?

dad

i think i'll cry myself
to sleep tonight
a bottle of barefoot
by my side

you should know
the pain you caused
won't melt away

the bite of this wine
reminds me that i'm here
to stay

i wish you knew
how much i really cared
and that i always wondered
why you weren't there